COLE'S COOKING COMPANION SERIES

MUFFINS
& OTHER
QUICK BREADS

D0043089

COLE GROUP

Both U.S. and metric units are provided for all recipes in this book. Ingredients are listed with U.S. units on the left and metric units on the right. The metric quantities have been rounded for ease of use; as a result, in some recipes there may be a slight difference (approximately ½ ounce or 15 grams) between the portion sizes for the two types of measurements.

© 1995 Cole Group, Inc.

Front cover photograph: Allan Rosenberg

Although every effort has been made at the time of publication to guarantee the accuracy of information sources and technical data, readers must assume responsibility for selection and use of suppliers and supplies.

Cole Group, the Cole colophon, and Cole's Cooking Companion are trademarks of Cole Publishing Group, Inc.

Cole Group, Inc.
1330 N. Dutton Ave., Suite 103
Santa Rosa, CA 95401
(800) 959-2717   (707) 526-2682
Fax (707) 526-2687

Printed in Hong Kong

G F E D C B A
1 0 9 8 7 6 5

ISBN 1-56426-811-X

Library of Congress Catalog Card Number 95-23971

Distributed to the book trade by Publishers Group West

Cole books are available for quantity purchases for sales promotions, premiums, fund-raising, or educational use. For more information on *Muffins & Other Quick Breads* or other Cole's Cooking Companion books, please write or call the publisher.

CONTENTS

QUICK FIX, QUICK BAKE

*T*ender muffins embellished with fruit and
nuts, currant-studded rounds sending up
fragrant plumes of steam, crisp-crusted
biscuits with flaky layers and a silky crumb—
all are quick breads, so named because you
make them from scratch in only minutes.
Muffins & Other Quick Breads shows just
how fast and easy "fresh-baked" can be.

RISING TO THE OCCASION

For breakfasts and brunches, coffee breaks and snacks, lunches, teatime, family suppers, even elegant dining—almost any occasion is a good time for quick breads. The virtues of this delectable family of breads have special appeal for busy people who love to bake: There's no lengthy kneading and no waiting for the dough to rise, so quick breads are in and out of the oven (or frying kettle) fast.

Unlike yeasted breads, quick breads use fast-acting leavening agents or steam to make them rise. Muffins, biscuits, and most other types of quick breads are leavened with baking powder and/or baking soda, while the steam from beaten eggs lightens popovers and baked goods made from cream puff dough.

The basic ingredients in muffins—flour, flavorings, perhaps some leavening, and liquid—are the same ones used in almost a dozen other varieties of quick breads. Creating such amazing diversity from a few common staples is largely a matter of adjusting the proportions of dry and liquid ingredients. Popovers, for example, are made from a thin batter with approximately equal parts of dry and liquid ingredients. Double the proportion of dry to liquid ingredients and you get a thicker batter that bakes up into muffins or loaves. Thicker still, with a ratio of dry to liquid ingredients approaching three to one, are soft doughs for cut biscuits, scones, and fry breads such as buñuelos.

BASICS FOR BREADS ON THE DOUBLE

The preparation techniques described in the following pages apply to muffins and most other batter-based quick breads.

Preparing the Oven and Pans Start by preheating the oven and positioning a rack in the center of the oven.

Unless otherwise specified, the muffin recipes in this book use a standard 12-hole muffin pan or two 6-hole pans with cups measuring about 2½ inches (6.25 cm) across the rim. The recipes for quick loaves use a 8½- by 4½- by 2½-inch (21.25- by 11.25- by 6.25-cm) pan. For all other recipes, use whatever pan size the recipe specifies.

Nonstick bakeware requires no special preparation; conventional bakeware needs a light coating of oil or butter. For muffin pans, coat the rims as well as the cups to reduce sticking. For quick loaves, breads, and cakes, lightly flour the oiled or buttered pans, then turn them upside down and tap the bottom to remove excess flour. The dusting of flour helps the batter rise during baking and gives the crust a professional-looking finish.

Mixing Ingredients and Filling Pans Measure the dry ingredients into a bowl and blend well. Purists recommend shaking the dry ingredients through a sifter or sieve several times to mix them thoroughly. Using a separate bowl, measure and blend the liquid ingredients.

To mix batters for most muffins and other quick breads made with melted butter or oil (like the Strawberry Ripple Tea Cake on page 62) pour the liquid mixture all at once into the dry ingredients, stirring just enough to barely moisten the ingredients. *Easy does it!* Unless the recipe directs you otherwise, resist the temptation to beat the batter smooth; it should be lumpy. Overmixing results in an uneven crust, a coarse-textured crumb with air tunnels, and other undesirable characteristics.

For most batters made with softened butter or shortening (like Sally Lunn, Georgia-Style on page 66), allow the fat to warm to room temperature, then cream it with sugar until light and fluffy before combining it with other ingredients. For biscuits, scones, and other dough-based quick breads made with chilled butter or shortening (like Irish Soda Bread on page 41), work the fat into the dry ingredients until the particles are the size of coarse crumbs, then add the liquid. For popovers, cream puff dough specialties, and fry breads, mix ingredients according to the instructions given in the recipe.

Fill prepared muffin cups no more than three-fourths full of batter (unless you're making the Monster Muffins on page 32). Fill prepared loaf or cake pans no more than two-thirds full and spread the batter evenly with a spatula before baking.

Baking and Cooling For maximum rising power, get the pans into the oven as soon as they are filled. Quick breads are done when the center of the top crust springs back when pressed lightly and a toothpick inserted into the middle comes out clean and dry, with no wet crumbs clinging to it.

Turn baked muffins and other quick breads onto a wire rack to cool. If the crust seems to stick, loosen it by lightly tapping the bottom of the pan. If that doesn't work, let the pan sit briefly on the rack. The steam produced as the contents cool may help free any areas that stick. As a last resort, run a knife blade around the edge to loosen the contents.

Storing and Reheating Muffins and most quick breads are at their best when eaten soon after baking. Those that contain fruit, nuts, vegetables, or moderately high amounts of fat stay moist longer than plain ones and those that are low in fat. If you have any leftover muffins that won't be eaten the same day they're made, don't put them in the refrigerator, where they will quickly dry out. Instead, store them in an airtight container and freeze for up to 12 months. To reheat, bake the frozen muffins, wrapped in aluminum foil, at 350°F (175°C) for 15–20 minutes, or until thawed and heated through. Biscuits and scones can be stored the same way as muffins. Fry breads do not store as well as other quick breads, but you can freeze them for up to a month.

Most quick loaves, breads, and cakes will stay fresh and moist three or four days at room temperature if they are carefully wrapped first in plastic wrap and then in aluminum foil. They freeze well for up to four months. To reheat, thaw them in their wrappings at room temperature, then unwrap, cover loosely with foil, and bake in a 350°F (175°C) oven for about 10 minutes.

RECIPES AND TECHNIQUES

*M*uffins, gems, quick loaves, corn breads, tea cakes, coffee rings, biscuits, shortcake, scones, popovers, cream puff pastries, and fry breads—these and other quick breads are enjoying a renaissance in contemporary cuisine. The recipes and techniques in *Muffins & Other Quick Breads* aptly demonstrate why good cooks everywhere are delighted to rediscover this family of delicious breads.

MUFFINS

The perfect muffin has a gently rounded top and golden crust; a moist, finely grained crumb; an appealing aroma and satisfying balance of flavors permeating every tender bite. In this section you'll find more than a baker's dozen tempting varieties that will keep muffin lovers coming back for more.

PINEAPPLE MUFFINS

These tropical fruit muffins stay fresh-tasting and tender for several days. To lower the fat content and create a lighter muffin, you can substitute four egg whites for the two whole eggs used in this recipe.

2½ cups	unbleached flour	600 ml
¾ cup	sugar	175 ml
1 tbl	baking powder	1 tbl
pinch	salt	pinch
⅓ cup	oil	85 ml
2	eggs	2
1 can (20 oz)	crushed pineapple in pineapple juice, undrained	1 can (570 g)

1. Preheat oven to 350°F (175°C). In a large bowl sift together flour, sugar, baking powder, and salt. Make well in center.

2. In a medium bowl mix together oil, eggs, pineapple and its juice and pour into well, stirring just until dry ingredients are moistened.

3. Fill prepared muffin pans two-thirds full. Bake until golden brown (25–30 minutes). Serve warm.

Makes 12 muffins.

APPLE-PECAN MUFFINS

Prepare a quick batch of these deliciously moist fruit-and-nut muffins for breakfast or a satisfying snack.

2 cups	unbleached flour	500 ml
⅓ cup	sugar	85 ml
1 tbl	baking powder	1 tbl
½ tsp	salt	½ tsp
½ tsp	ground cinnamon	½ tsp
½ cup	finely chopped pecans	125 ml
1	egg	1
1 cup	milk	250 ml
3 tbl	butter, melted and cooled, or oil	3 tbl
1	apple, shredded	1

1. Preheat oven to 400°F (205°C). In a large bowl stir together flour, sugar, baking powder, salt, cinnamon, and ¼ cup (60 ml) of the pecans. Make well in center.

2. In a medium bowl beat egg with milk and melted butter. Stir in apple. Pour egg mixture into flour mixture, stirring just until dry ingredients are moistened.

3. Fill prepared muffin pans two-thirds full. Sprinkle each muffin lightly with remaining pecans. Bake until well browned (25–30 minutes). Serve warm or at room temperature.

Makes 12 muffins.

CARROT-GINGER MUFFINS

Once considered dessert, carrot cake takes a new twist: Add freshly grated ginger to the batter, bake it in muffin pans, and serve the spicy-sweet muffins with eggs Benedict for breakfast in bed.

2 cups	unbleached flour	500 ml
1 tbl	baking powder	1 tbl
1 tsp	baking soda	1 tsp
½ tsp	salt	½ tsp
½ tsp	ground nutmeg	½ tsp
½ tsp	ground cinnamon	½ tsp
2 tsp	freshly grated ginger	2 tsp
½ cup	yogurt or buttermilk	125 ml
¼ cup	oil	60 ml
¼ cup	maple syrup	60 ml
¼ cup	honey	60 ml
3	eggs	3
2 cups	grated carrot	500 ml

1. Preheat oven to 400°F (205°C). In a large bowl combine flour, baking powder, baking soda, salt, nutmeg, and cinnamon.

2. In a separate bowl combine ginger, yogurt, oil, maple syrup, honey, and eggs. Stir together contents of both bowls, then stir in carrots.

3. Fill prepared muffin pans three-fourths full. Bake until lightly browned (15–18 minutes). Serve warm.

Makes 12 muffins.

MAPLE-NUT BRAN MUFFINS

These layered bran muffins include a luxurious touch—real maple sugar, produced by boiling maple sap beyond the syrup stage until the liquid evaporates and crystals form. If maple sugar is not available where you live, substitute brown sugar.

Maple-Nut Filling

½ cup	firmly packed maple or brown sugar	125 ml
½ cup	finely chopped walnuts	125 ml
2 tbl	unbleached flour	2 tbl
½ tsp	ground cinnamon	½ tsp
1 cup	whole-bran cereal	250 ml
¾ cup	milk	175 ml
1	egg	1
¼ cup	butter, melted and cooled, or oil	60 ml
1 cup	unbleached flour	250 ml
2½ tsp	baking powder	2½ tsp
½ tsp	salt	½ tsp
¼ cup	sugar	60 ml

1. To make filling, in a medium bowl combine maple sugar, walnuts, flour, and cinnamon. Blend well and set aside.

2. Preheat oven to 400°F (205°C). In a medium bowl combine cereal and milk; let stand until most of the liquid is absorbed (about 10 minutes). Beat in egg and melted butter.

3. In a large bowl mix remaining ingredients. Add cereal mixture, mixing just until dry ingredients are moistened. Spoon a small amount of batter into each cup of a prepared muffin pan; sprinkle with some of the filling. Repeat layers until cups are about three-fourths full.

4. Bake until muffins are well browned (20–25 minutes). Serve warm.

Makes 12 muffins.

HONEY-BRAN MUFFINS

Bursting with plump raisins, these honey-sweetened bran muffins make a hearty breakfast bread.

1 cup	whole-bran cereal	250 ml
½ cup each	milk and honey	125 ml each
1	egg	1
¼ cup	butter, melted and cooled, or oil	60 ml
½ cup	raisins	125 ml
1 cup	unbleached flour	250 ml
2½ tsp	baking powder	2½ tsp
¼ tsp	salt	¼ tsp

1. Preheat oven to 400°F (205°C). In a medium bowl combine cereal, milk, and honey; let stand until most of the liquid is absorbed (about 10 minutes). Beat in egg and melted butter, then mix in raisins.

2. In a large bowl combine remaining ingredients. Add cereal mixture, mixing just until dry ingredients are moistened.

3. Fill prepared muffin pans about two-thirds full. Bake until well browned (20–25 minutes). Serve warm.

Makes 12 muffins.

USING BUTTER IN QUICK BREADS

Nothing gives baked goods a rich flavor and tender crumb like real butter. Softened butter, which produces a delicate, cakelike texture, is prepared by letting butter stand at room temperature until it is soft enough to be easily worked with a spoon. Melted butter, which can be used interchangeably with oil in many quick bread recipes, is made by warming butter over low heat until it liquifies but is not yet browned.

LEMON-POPPY SEED MUFFINS

Fragrant and buttery, these muffins won't last long around hungry guests and family members.

1½ cups	unbleached flour	350 ml
2 tsp	baking powder	2 tsp
½ tsp	baking soda	½ tsp
pinch	salt	pinch
1 tbl	grated lemon zest	1 tbl
¼ cup	poppy seed	60 ml
½ cup	butter, softened	125 ml
¾ cup	sugar	175 ml
2	eggs	2
1 tsp	vanilla extract	1 tsp
⅔ cup	milk	150 ml

1. Preheat oven to 350°F (175°C). In a medium bowl mix flour, baking powder, baking soda, salt, lemon zest, and poppy seed together and set aside.

2. In a large bowl cream softened butter and sugar together until light, fluffy, and a pale, ivory color. Add eggs, one at a time, beating well after each addition (if mixture begins to curdle as you mix in eggs, add 1 tablespoon flour and beat on low speed until blended). Stir in vanilla and milk. Fold in dry ingredients, blending just until dry ingredients are moistened.

3. Fill prepared muffin pans three-fourths full. Bake until golden brown (20–25 minutes). Serve warm.

Makes 12 muffins.

STRAWBERRY-FILLED MUFFINS

Hidden inside each muffin is a flavorful pocket of strawberry jam. Raspberry, blueberry, or peach preserves work equally well.

2 cups	unbleached flour	500 ml
¼ cup	sugar	60 ml
1 tbl	baking powder	1 tbl
½ tsp	salt	½ tsp
⅛ tsp	ground nutmeg	⅛ tsp
1	egg	1
1 cup	milk	250 ml
3 tbl	butter, melted and cooled, or oil	3 tbl
⅓ cup	strawberry jam	85 ml

1. Preheat oven to 400°F (205°C). In a large bowl stir together flour, sugar, baking powder, salt, and nutmeg. Make well in center.

2. In a medium bowl beat egg with milk and melted butter. Pour egg mixture into flour mixture, stirring just until dry ingredients are moistened.

3. Fill prepared muffin pans about one-third full, using half the batter. To each muffin cup, add about 1 teaspoon strawberry jam. Use remaining batter to fill pans two-thirds full.

4. Bake until well browned (20–25 minutes). Serve warm.

Makes 12 muffins.

BLUEBERRY-STREUSEL MUFFINS

With a spiced crumb topping, these blueberry muffins (see photo on page 25) are like miniature coffee cakes.

Butter Crumb Topping

⅓ cup each	unbleached flour and sugar	85 ml each
¼ tsp	ground cinnamon	¼ tsp
¼ cup	butter, chilled	60 ml
2 cups	unbleached flour	500 ml
¼ cup	sugar	60 ml
1 tbl	baking powder	1 tbl
½ tsp	salt	½ tsp
¼ tsp	ground nutmeg	¼ tsp
1	egg	1
1 cup	milk	250 ml
3 tbl	butter, melted and cooled, or oil	3 tbl
1 cup	fresh blueberries	250 ml

1. To make crumb topping, in a small bowl mix together flour, sugar, and cinnamon. Cut in butter until coarse crumbs form. Set aside.

2. Preheat oven to 400°F (205°C). In a large bowl stir together flour, sugar, baking powder, salt, and nutmeg. Make a well in center.

3. In a medium bowl beat egg with milk and melted butter. Pour egg mixture into flour mixture, stirring just until dry ingredients are moistened. Gently fold in blueberries.

4. Fill prepared muffin pans about three-fourths full. Sprinkle tops evenly with crumb topping. Bake until well browned (25–30 minutes). Serve warm.

Makes 12 muffins.

ORANGE-RAISIN MUFFINS

The basic raisin muffin is elevated to new heights with a hint of orange zest pervading every bite.

2 cups	unbleached flour	500 ml
¼ cup	sugar	60 ml
1 tbl	baking powder	1 tbl
½ tsp	salt	½ tsp
½ cup	raisins	125 ml
1	egg	1
1 cup	milk	250 ml
3 tbl	butter, melted and cooled, or oil	3 tbl
2 tsp	grated orange zest	2 tsp

1. Preheat oven to 400°F (205°C). In a large bowl stir together flour, sugar, baking powder, salt, and raisins. Make well in center.

2. In a medium bowl beat egg with milk, melted butter, and orange zest. Add egg mixture to flour mixture, stirring just until dry ingredients are moistened.

3. Fill prepared muffin pans about two-thirds full. Bake until well browned (20–25 minutes). Serve warm.

Makes 12 muffins.

ADDING FRESH FRUIT TO BATTER

Whole berries and chopped fresh fruit are less likely to sink to the bottom of muffins and other quick breads during baking if you dredge them in flour, then shake off the excess flour in a colander before adding them to the batter. Besides helping to suspend the fruit evenly throughout the batter, the flour coating keeps moist pieces of fruit from clumping together.

CRANBERRY-SPICE MUFFINS

Tart cranberries, cinnamon, and nutmeg flavor a splendidly colorful and nutritious muffin that is especially good for brunch or Sunday supper.

¾ cup	fresh cranberries, coarsely chopped	175 ml
½ cup	sugar	125 ml
2 cups	unbleached flour	500 ml
1 tbl	baking powder	1 tbl
½ tsp	salt	½ tsp
½ tsp	ground cinnamon	½ tsp
¼ tsp	ground nutmeg	¼ tsp
1	egg	1
1 cup	milk	250 ml
3 tbl	butter, melted and cooled, or oil	3 tbl
2 tsp	grated orange zest	2 tsp

1. In a small bowl mix together cranberries and ⅓ cup (85 ml) of the sugar. Set aside.

2. Preheat oven to 400°F (205°C). In a large bowl stir together flour, remaining sugar, baking powder, salt, cinnamon, and nutmeg. Make well in center.

3. In a medium bowl beat egg with milk, melted butter, and orange zest. Pour egg mixture into flour mixture, stirring just until dry ingredients are moistened, adding cranberry mixture with last few strokes.

4. Fill prepared muffin pans two-thirds full. Bake until well browned (25–30 minutes). Serve warm.

Makes 12 muffins.

CINNAMON-CURRANT MINI MUFFINS

These tiny two-bite miniatures make perfect tea cakes or snacks for children. To make a dozen full-size muffins, substitute a standard 12-hole muffin pan.

Cinnamon Sugar

½ cup	sugar	125 ml
1 tsp	ground cinnamon	1 tsp
1½ cups	unbleached flour	350 ml
1½ tsp	baking powder	1½ tsp
¼ tsp each	salt and ground nutmeg	¼ tsp each
¼ cup	dried currants	60 ml
⅓ cup	butter, softened	85 ml
½ cup	sugar	125 ml
½ tsp	vanilla extract	½ tsp
1	egg	1
½ cup	milk	125 ml
¼ cup	butter, melted and cooled	60 ml

1. In a small bowl combine sugar and cinnamon. Set aside.

2. Preheat oven to 375°F (190°C). In a medium bowl mix flour, baking powder, salt, nutmeg, and currants.

3. In a large mixing bowl cream ⅓ cup (85 ml) of the softened butter with sugar, then beat in vanilla and egg until well combined. Add flour mixture to butter mixture alternately with milk, mixing after each addition just until lightly combined.

4. Fill prepared 1¾-inch (4.4-cm) miniature muffin pans two-thirds full. Bake until muffins are golden brown (18–20 minutes). Remove hot muffins from pans and dip quickly into melted butter. Roll in Cinnamon Sugar to coat. Serve warm.

Makes 24 mini muffins.

OATMEAL GEMS

The name "gem" refers to the old-fashioned cast-iron pans traditionally used to produce a crusty exterior and a pointy top on these molasses-sweetened muffins (see photo on page 11). If you don't have a gem pan, use a regular muffin pan.

2 cups	quick-cooking oatmeal	500 ml
1½ cups	buttermilk	350 ml
¼ cup	molasses	60 ml
2 tbl	sugar	2 tbl
2	eggs	2
½ tsp	salt	½ tsp
1 cup	unbleached flour	250 ml
1 tsp	baking soda	1 tsp

1. Preheat oven to 400°F (205°C). Combine oatmeal and buttermilk in a medium bowl and let stand about 15 minutes.

2. Beat in molasses, sugar, eggs, and salt. Stir flour and baking soda together, then add to oatmeal mixture and mix just until dry ingredients are moistened.

3. Fill prepared gem or muffin pans two-thirds full. Bake until golden brown (about 20 minutes). Serve warm.

Makes about 16 gems or 12 muffins.

MONSTER MUFFINS

On the assumption that you can't have too much of a good thing, many bake shops offer muffins of huge proportions, some as large as 4 inches (10 cm) across. You can transform most muffins in this section into giants by filling standard muffin cups all the way to the rim with batter. Be sure to oil the rims and top surfaces of the pan as well as the muffin cups. Increase baking time by 10–12 minutes, and check for doneness after 20 minutes, then every 10 minutes.

Lemon-Currant Muffins

A sprinkling of lemon zest and sugar creates a pebbly, tart-sweet crust on these golden currant muffins.

Lemon Sugar

2 tsp	grated lemon zest	2 tsp
1/3 cup	sugar	85 ml
2 cups	unbleached flour	500 ml
1/4 cup	sugar	60 ml
1 tbl	baking powder	1 tbl
1/2 tsp	salt	1/2 tsp
1/8 tsp	ground mace or ground nutmeg	1/8 tsp
1/4 cup	dried currants	60 ml
1	egg	1
1 cup	milk	250 ml
3 tbl	butter, melted and cooled, or oil	3 tbl
1 tbl each	grated lemon zest and lemon juice	1 tbl each

1. In a small bowl combine lemon zest and sugar. Mix well, crushing lemon zest with a spoon to release oils into sugar. Set aside.

2. Preheat oven to 400° (205°C). In a large bowl stir together flour, sugar, baking powder, salt, mace, and currants. Make well in center.

3. In a medium bowl beat egg with remaining ingredients. Pour egg mixture into flour mixture, stirring just until dry ingredients are moistened.

4. Fill prepared muffin pans two-thirds full. Sprinkle tops evenly with Lemon Sugar. Bake until well browned (20–25 minutes). Serve warm.

Makes 12 muffins.

TUSCAN HERB MUFFINS

Thyme, basil, and oregano combine with Parmesan cheese to make a savory muffin that pairs nicely with a hearty bowl of soup or a crisp salad.

2 cups	unbleached flour	500 ml
1 tbl	baking powder	1 tbl
1 tsp	baking soda	1 tsp
½ tsp	salt	½ tsp
1 tsp	dried oregano	1 tsp
1 tsp	dried thyme	1 tsp
1 tsp	dried basil	1 tsp
2	eggs	2
1	egg white	1
1 cup	buttermilk	250 ml
4 tbl	olive oil	4 tbl
1 tbl	honey	1 tbl
¼ cup	grated Parmesan cheese	60 ml

1. Preheat oven to 400°F (205°C). In a large bowl combine flour, baking powder, baking soda, salt, oregano, thyme, and basil.

2. In a separate bowl combine eggs, egg white, buttermilk, oil, honey, and Parmesan cheese. Pour egg mixture into flour mixture, stirring just until dry ingredients are moistened.

3. Fill prepared muffin pans two-thirds full. Bake for 25 minutes. Let cool slightly.

Makes 12 muffins.

CHEDDAR MUFFINS

Golden cheese muffins, capped with sesame seeds, make a robust accompaniment to omelets or soups.

2 cups	unbleached flour	500 ml
2 tbl	sugar	2 tbl
1 tbl	baking powder	1 tbl
½ tsp	salt	½ tsp
1 cup	grated sharp Cheddar cheese	250 ml
1	egg	1
1 cup	milk	250 ml
3 tbl	butter, melted and cooled, or oil	3 tbl
as needed	sesame seeds (optional)	as needed

1. Preheat oven to 400°F (205°C). In a large bowl stir together flour, sugar, baking powder, salt, and Cheddar cheese. Make well in center.

2. In a medium bowl beat egg with milk and melted butter. Add egg mixture to flour mixture, stirring just until dry ingredients are moistened.

3. Fill prepared muffin pans two-thirds full. Sprinkle each muffin lightly with sesame seeds. Bake until well browned (20–25 minutes). Serve warm.

Makes 12 muffins.

MUFFIN SAVORIES

Muffins needn't always be sweet, as the recipes for Tuscan Herb Muffins and Cheddar Muffins (see pages 34 and 36) prove so aptly. For other varieties of muffins with a savory flavor, try substituting any one of the following ingredients for the Cheddar cheese in the recipe on page 36:

- *6–8 slices bacon, cooked and crumbled*
- *3 tablespoons chopped cooked ham*
- *¼ cup grated Parmesan cheese*
- *⅓ cup crumbled Roquefort cheese*
- *2 tablespoons finely chopped parsley or chives*
- *2 teaspoons finely chopped fresh sage*

EASY CORNMEAL MUFFIN MIX

This big-batch muffin mix is a snap to make and stores well in a cupboard or freezer until ready to use. Made with butter, it can be stored in a freezer up to four months. Made with shortening, it can be stored in a cupboard up to six months and is ideal for camping. Add your favorite chopped nuts or grated cheese for variety.

To use muffin mix for preparing a single batch of 12 muffins, measure out 2⅓ cups (585 ml) muffin mix. Then in a separate bowl beat an egg with 1 cup (250 ml) milk. Quickly blend dry and liquid ingredients just until dry ingredients are moistened. Fill prepared muffin or corn stick pans two-thirds full and bake in a preheated oven at 425°F (220°C) for 12–18 minutes.

4 cups	cornmeal	900 ml
4 cups	flour	900 ml
¾ cup	sugar	175 ml
¼ cup	baking powder	60 ml
2¼ tsp	salt	2¼ tsp
1 cup	butter or shortening, chilled	250 ml

1. In a large bowl combine cornmeal, flour, sugar, baking powder, and salt; stir to blend. Cut in butter with a pastry blender or two knives until mixture resembles fine meal.

2. Store mixture in a large plastic bag or divide into four 2⅓-cup (585-ml) portions until ready to use.

Makes 48 muffins or corn sticks.

LOAVES, BREADS, AND CAKES

Spread with cream cheese or butter, or served unadorned, quick loaves, breads, and cakes make a marvelous accompaniment to tea or coffee, a welcome addition to a meal, or a gracious gift. From traditional steamed brown bread to an updated version of gingerbread, this section offers the best of classic and new-fashioned quick bread specialties.

IRISH SODA BREAD

This currant-filled round is like a giant biscuit. The distinctive appearance of the top crust is formed by slashing an x into the dough before baking. Serve the soda bread sliced, with fresh butter and marmalade.

3 cups	unbleached flour	700 ml
3 tbl	sugar	3 tbl
1 tsp each	baking soda and baking powder	1 tsp each
½ tsp	salt	½ tsp
3 tbl	butter, chilled	3 tbl
½ cup	dried currants or raisins	125 ml
1¼ cups	buttermilk	300 ml
2 tsp	milk	2 tsp

1. Preheat oven to 375°F (190°C). In a large bowl stir together flour, sugar, baking soda, baking powder, and salt. Cut in butter until coarse crumbs form. Stir in currants.

2. Add buttermilk and stir just until dry ingredients are moistened.

3. Turn dough out onto a floured surface and shape into a flattened ball about 1½ inches (3.75 cm) high. Place on an oiled baking sheet and brush with milk. With a floured knife cut an *x* into top of loaf (cutting from center to within about 1 inch or 2.5 cm of edge) about ¼ inch (.6 cm) deep.

4. Bake until loaf is golden brown (40–45 minutes). Slide loaf onto a wire rack to cool slightly. Cut into thick slices and serve warm.

Makes 1 loaf.

BOSTON BROWN BREAD

Dark and sweet with raisins and molasses, this old-fashioned steamed bread is customarily served on weekends in New England with a big pot of baked beans. Steam the bread in a cylindrical mold, a coffee can, or two fruit or vegetable cans.

½ cup each	rye flour, whole wheat flour, and cornmeal	125 ml each
1¼ tsp	baking soda	1¼ tsp
½ tsp	salt	½ tsp
1 cup	buttermilk	250 ml
⅓ cup	molasses	85 ml
½ cup	raisins	125 ml

1. Have ready several quarts of water boiling. In a medium bowl stir and toss together flours, cornmeal, baking soda, and salt.

2. Stir together buttermilk and molasses, add to dry ingredients along with raisins, and stir thoroughly.

3. Pour batter into a prepared 1-pound (450-g) coffee can or divide it equally between two 1-pound (450-g) fruit or vegetable cans about 3 inches (7.5 cm) in diameter and 4–5 inches (10–12.5 cm) high. Cover tops tightly with aluminum foil.

4. Place mold or can(s) in kettle on a rack and pour in boiling water to come halfway up the sides. Cover kettle and set over low heat, maintaining a low boil. Steam for about 2 hours if using mold or coffee can, or about 1½ hours if using smaller cans.

5. Remove mold or can(s) from water, let stand 5 minutes, then unmold onto a rack to cool completely before slicing.

Makes 1 large or 2 small loaves.

NEW-FASHIONED GINGERBREAD

Assemble the batter and put it in the microwave just as you sit down for dinner. The gingerbread will bake, stand the required time, and be ready to serve by the time you're ready for dessert.

2	eggs, beaten	2
⅓ cup	sugar	85 ml
½ cup	oil	125 ml
⅓ cup	dark molasses	85 ml
1 tsp	baking powder	1 tsp
½ tsp	baking soda	½ tsp
½ tsp	salt	½ tsp
1½ tsp	ground ginger	1½ tsp
½ tsp	ground cloves	½ tsp
½ tsp	ground cinnamon	½ tsp
1½ cups	unbleached flour	350 ml
½ cup	sour cream	125 ml
as needed	sweetened whipped cream (optional)	as needed

1. In a large mixing bowl combine eggs, sugar, oil, and molasses; stir until well blended. Stir in baking powder, baking soda, salt, ginger, cloves, and cinnamon, mixing thoroughly. Add flour alternately with sour cream. Stir just until well blended.

2. Pour batter into a prepared 9-inch-square (22.5-cm-square) dish and smooth top. Microwave on full power until top appears dry and cake loosens from sides of dish (7–9 minutes). Remove from microwave. Let stand directly on heatproof surface 10 minutes. Cut into 3-inch (7.5-cm) squares and serve warm with whipped cream, if desired.

Makes 9 squares.

FRENCH HONEY-SPICE BREAD

This holiday loaf contains neither butter nor oil.

1 cup	coarsely chopped almonds	250 ml
½ cup	golden raisins	125 ml
½ tsp	salt	½ tsp
¼ tsp	ground nutmeg	¼ tsp
1 tsp each	ground ginger, ground cinnamon, and ground anise seed	1 tsp each
pinch	ground cloves	pinch
1 tsp	baking powder	1 tsp
2 tsp each	baking soda and freshly grated orange zest	2 tsp each
1 cup each	water and honey	250 ml each
¼ cup	firmly packed brown sugar	60 ml
1	egg, lightly beaten	1
⅓ cup	dark rum	85 ml
1 cup each	rye flour, whole wheat flour, and bread flour	250 ml each

1. Preheat oven to 400°F (205°C). In a large bowl combine almonds, raisins, salt, nutmeg, ginger, cinnamon, anise seed, cloves, baking powder, baking soda and orange zest.

2. In a medium saucepan, bring the water to a boil. Add honey and sugar and stir to dissolve. Remove from heat; cool 5 minutes. Add egg and rum to honey-sugar mixture and whisk to blend. Add to spice mixture and stir to blend. Add flours and stir just until dry ingredients are moistened.

3. Transfer batter to a prepared standard size loaf pan and bake 10 minutes. Reduce heat to 350°F (175°C) and bake until bread is dark brown (about 30 more minutes). Cool in pan on a rack for 5 minutes. Unmold and finish cooling. Wrap tightly in plastic wrap, then store at room temperature 2–3 days.

Makes 1 loaf.

CHOCOLATE CHIP-ORANGE BREAD

Chocolate and orange flavors enhance this sweet loaf (see photo on page 9) that's good spread with cream cheese.

2 cups	unbleached flour	500 ml
2 tsp	baking powder	2 tsp
½ tsp	salt	½ tsp
¼ tsp	baking soda	¼ tsp
½ cup	sugar	125 ml
½ cup	chopped walnuts	125 ml
one 6-oz pkg (1 cup)	semisweet chocolate chips	one 170-g pkg (250 ml)
2	eggs	2
¼ cup	milk	60 ml
½ cup	orange juice	125 ml
2 tsp	grated orange zest	2 tsp
1 tsp	vanilla extract	1 tsp
⅓ cup	butter, melted and cooled, or oil	85 ml

1. Preheat oven to 350°F (175°C). In a large bowl stir together flour, baking powder, salt, baking soda, and sugar. Mix in walnuts and ¾ cup (175 ml) of the chocolate chips. Make well in center.

2. In a medium bowl beat eggs with milk, orange juice, orange zest, and vanilla; then blend in butter. Pour egg mixture into flour mixture, mixing just until dry ingredients are moistened.

3. Spread batter in a prepared standard size loaf pan. Sprinkle evenly with remaining chocolate chips. Bake until golden brown (55–60 minutes). Let cool in pan for 10 minutes, then turn out onto a wire rack to cool completely.

Makes 1 loaf.

Harvest Bread

Spicy and rich, this autumn bread makes a fine partner for soups or baked beans.

2 cups	unbleached flour	500 ml
2 tsp	baking powder	2 tsp
1 tsp	ground cinnamon	1 tsp
½ tsp	ground nutmeg	½ tsp
¼ tsp each	salt, baking soda, ground ginger, and ground cloves	¼ tsp each
¼ cup	sugar	60 ml
½ cup	chopped walnuts	125 ml
¼ cup	raisins	60 ml
2	eggs, lightly beaten	2
½ cup	firmly packed brown sugar	125 ml
1 cup	cooked, puréed acorn or butternut squash	250 ml
½ tsp	vanilla extract	½ tsp
⅓ cup	butter, melted and cooled, or oil	85 ml

1. Preheat oven to 350°F (175°C). In a large bowl stir together flour, baking powder, cinnamon, nutmeg, salt, baking soda, ginger, cloves, and sugar. Mix in walnuts and raisins. Make well in center.

2. In a medium mixing bowl beat eggs with brown sugar, squash, vanilla, and butter. Add squash mixture to flour mixture, mixing just until dry ingredients are moistened.

3. Spread batter in a prepared standard size loaf pan. Bake until loaf is well browned (50–55 minutes). Let cool in pan for 10 minutes, then turn out onto a wire rack to cool completely.

Makes 1 loaf.

Pumpkin-Spice Loaf

Pumpkins are not just for Halloween or Thanksgiving, as this bread demonstrates. The combination of cooked pumpkin purée and aromatic spices in a whole wheat and oatmeal batter makes an irresistibly healthy loaf. Serve with hot mulled cider.

1½ cups	unbleached flour	350 ml
½ cup	oatmeal or oat flour	125 ml
2 tsp	baking powder	2 tsp
2 tsp	baking soda	2 tsp
2 tsp	ground cinnamon	2 tsp
2 tsp	ground nutmeg	2 tsp
¼ tsp	ground allspice	¼ tsp
2 tsp	freshly grated ginger	2 tsp
½ cup	maple syrup	125 ml
¼ cup	molasses	60 ml
¼ cup	butter, melted and cooled, or oil	60 ml
2	egg whites	2
1	egg	1
2 tbl	lemon juice	2 tbl
1 tbl	grated orange zest	1 tbl
1 cup	canned pumpkin or cooked pumpkin purée	250 ml

1. Preheat oven to 350°F (175°C). In a large mixing bowl combine flour, oatmeal, baking powder, baking soda, cinnamon, nutmeg, and allspice. Make well in center.

2. In a medium mixing bowl thoroughly blend remaining ingredients. Combine contents of both bowls, mixing just until dry ingredients are moistened.

3. Pour mixture into a prepared standard size loaf pan. Bake until well browned (50–60 minutes). Let cool completely before slicing.

Makes 1 loaf.

SOUTHERN CORN BREAD

Light and crumbly, this golden corn bread from the South should be served fresh from the oven with butter and warmed honey. For a perfectly browned bottom crust, bake it in a cast-iron skillet.

1 cup	cornmeal	250 ml
1 cup	unbleached flour	250 ml
3 tbl	sugar	3 tbl
4 tsp	baking powder	4 tsp
½ tsp	salt	½ tsp
⅓ cup	butter, softened	85 ml
1	egg	1
1 cup	buttermilk	250 ml

1. Preheat oven to 400°F (205°C). Oil a 10-inch (25-cm) cast-iron skillet (or an 8- by 8-inch/20- by 20-cm baking pan) and place in oven to heat.

2. In a large bowl stir together cornmeal, flour, sugar, baking powder, and salt. Using a pastry blender, or two knives, cut in butter to make a coarse but even meal. Make well in center.

3. In a medium bowl beat together egg and buttermilk and pour into cornmeal mixture. Stir just until dry ingredients are moistened.

4. Pour mixture into preheated skillet. Bake until top is lightly browned and corn bread shrinks from the sides of the skillet (about 25 minutes). Serve warm.

Makes 8 large wedges or 16 squares.

JALAPEÑO CORN BREAD

Spicy bits of jalapeño chiles, corn kernels, and minced red onion give color and texture to plain corn bread. Try this corn bread for your next picnic or fireside supper. When available, red jalapeño chiles are an attractive addition.

1 cup	fresh or canned corn kernels	250 ml
2	green jalapeño chiles, minced	2
1	red onion, minced	1
1 cup	milk	250 ml
2	eggs	2
4 tbl	butter, melted and cooled, or oil	4 tbl
1 cup	unbleached flour	250 ml
1½ tsp each	baking powder, salt, and sugar	1½ tsp each
1 cup	cornmeal	250 ml
2 oz	Cheddar cheese, grated	60 g

1. Preheat oven to 400°F (205°C). In a medium mixing bowl combine corn, chiles, and onion. In a small bowl combine milk, eggs, and melted butter, then add to the corn mixture.

2. Sift together flour, baking powder, salt, and sugar. Stir in cornmeal. Gradually stir flour mixture and Cheddar cheese into the corn mixture just until combined and slightly lumpy. Do not stir until smooth or corn bread will be tough.

3. Spread mixture in a prepared 8-inch-square (20-cm-square) pan. Bake until top is golden brown (35–40 minutes). Cut into squares and serve.

Makes 16 squares.

ZUCCHINI-WALNUT BREAD

This flavorful version of a favorite quick bread will put a bountiful zucchini crop to good use. Freeze the extra loaf (see page 10).

3 cups	unbleached flour	700 ml
1 tbl	baking powder	1 tbl
1 tsp	salt	1 tsp
½ tsp each	ground cinnamon, ground nutmeg, and ground cloves	½ tsp each
¼ tsp	ground allspice	¼ tsp
½ cup	milk	125 ml
2	eggs, lightly beaten	2
½ cup	oil	125 ml
1½ cups	firmly packed brown sugar	350 ml
2½ cups	grated zucchini	600 ml
2 cups	chopped walnuts	500 ml

1. Preheat oven to 350°F (175°C). In a large bowl sift together flour, baking powder, salt, cinnamon, nutmeg, cloves, and allspice. Make well in center.

2. In a small bowl combine milk, eggs, oil, and sugar; pour into dry ingredients, stirring just until dry ingredients are moistened. Add zucchini and walnuts, and stir just to combine.

3. Divide batter evenly between two prepared standard size loaf pans. Bake until well browned (about 1 hour). Cool in pans for 15 minutes, then turn out onto a wire rack to cool completely.

Makes 2 loaves.

APRICOT-BANANA BREAD

A slice of this sweet bread reveals a colorful mosaic of fruit and nuts.

2 cups	unbleached flour	500 ml
1 tsp	baking powder	1 tsp
½ tsp each	baking soda and salt	½ tsp each
1 cup	sugar	250 ml
⅔ cup	chopped dried apricots	150 ml
½ cup	chopped walnuts	125 ml
1	egg	1
½ cup	milk	125 ml
1 tbl	walnut oil	1 tbl
1 tbl	oil	1 tbl
1	ripe banana, mashed	1

1. Preheat oven to 350°F (175°C). In a large bowl stir together flour, baking powder, baking soda, salt, and sugar. Mix in apricots and walnuts. Make well in center.

2. In a medium bowl beat egg with milk and oils. Blend in banana. Add banana mixture to flour mixture, stirring just until dry ingredients are moistened.

3. Spread batter in a prepared standard size loaf pan. Bake until loaf is well browned (65–70 minutes). Let cool in pan for 10 minutes, then turn out onto a rack to cool completely.

Makes 1 loaf.

QUICK BREADS AT YOUR CONVENIENCE

Most quick breads can be started several hours ahead of time and then baked at your convenience. Using separate bowls, measure and blend the dry and liquid ingredients, then cover and store in the refrigerator. When it's convenient, combine the dry and liquid mixtures with a few quick strokes and bake as usual.

BLUEBERRY-PECAN LOAF

Dimpled with blueberries and rich with pecans, this loaf is so sweet it can double as dessert.

2 cups	unbleached flour	500 ml
2 tsp	baking powder	2 tsp
½ tsp	salt	½ tsp
¼ tsp	baking soda	¼ tsp
¼ tsp	ground nutmeg	¼ tsp
½ cup	sugar	125 ml
½ cup	chopped pecans	125 ml
2	eggs	2
¼ cup	milk	60 ml
½ cup	orange juice	125 ml
2 tsp	grated orange zest	2 tsp
⅓ cup	butter, melted and cooled, or oil	85 ml
1 cup	fresh blueberries	250 ml

1. Preheat oven to 350°F (175°C). In a large bowl stir together flour, baking powder, salt, baking soda, nutmeg, and sugar. Mix in pecans. Make well in center.

2. In a medium bowl beat eggs with milk, orange juice, and orange zest; blend in melted butter. Add egg mixture to flour mixture, mixing just until dry ingredients are moistened. Gently fold in blueberries.

3. Spread batter in a prepared standard size loaf pan. Bake until loaf is golden brown (55–65 minutes). Let cool in pan for 10 minutes, then turn out onto a wire rack to cool completely.

Makes 1 loaf.

LEMON TEA BREAD

Lemon breads have always been a favorite at teatime. This sweet bread (see photo on page 77) tastes even better if carefully wrapped in foil or plastic wrap and allowed to rest for 12 hours before serving. It also freezes well (see page 10).

3 cups	unbleached flour	700 ml
1 tbl	baking powder	1 tbl
1 tsp	salt	1 tsp
½ cup	butter, softened	125 ml
1 cup	sugar	250 ml
1 tbl	finely grated lemon zest	1 tbl
2	eggs	2
1 cup	milk	250 ml
½ cup	fresh lemon juice	125 ml
1 tbl	vanilla extract	1 tbl

1. Preheat oven to 350°F (175°C). In a medium bowl sift together flour, baking powder, and salt.

2. In a large mixing bowl cream softened butter and sugar until light and fluffy; add zest and beat until a pale, ivory color. Add eggs, one at a time, beating well after each addition.

3. In a small bowl combine milk, lemon juice, and vanilla. To creamed butter mixture, gently stir in flour mixture alternately with the liquid, adding one third of each at a time; don't overmix batter.

4. Divide batter evenly between two prepared standard size loaf pans. Bake until golden brown (about 1 hour). Cool in pans for 15 minutes, then turn out onto a wire rack to cool completely.

Makes 2 loaves.

PULL-APART COFFEE RING

Biscuit dough makes a fine coffee ring (see photo on page 83).

¼ cup	butter, melted and cooled	60 ml
⅔ cup	firmly packed brown sugar	150 ml
2 cups	unbleached flour	500 ml
2 tbl	sugar	2 tbl
½ tsp	salt	½ tsp
¼ tsp	ground nutmeg	¼ tsp
2½ tsp	baking powder	2½ tsp
1 tbl	grated orange zest	1 tbl
¼ cup	butter, chilled	60 ml
1	egg	1
½ cup	milk	125 ml
¼ cup	finely chopped pecans	60 ml

1. Preheat oven to 400°F (205°C). Pour about 3 tablespoons of the melted butter into an 8-inch (20-cm) ring mold. Sprinkle with ⅓ cup (85 ml) of the brown sugar; set mold aside.

2. In a large bowl mix flour, sugar, salt, nutmeg, baking powder, and half of the orange zest. Cut in chilled butter until coarse crumbs form.

3. In a small bowl beat egg with milk until blended. Add egg mixture to flour mixture, stirring just until mixture clings together. Turn out on a floured surface and shape into a ball. In a separate bowl mix remaining brown sugar, remaining orange zest, and pecans.

4. Pinch off walnut-sized pieces of dough, shape into balls, and dip in remaining melted butter. Arrange a layer of dough balls, spaced slightly apart, in prepared ring mold. Sprinkle evenly with pecan mixture. Place remaining dough balls over first layer. Drizzle with any remaining butter. Bake until golden (25–30 minutes). Invert onto a serving plate and let stand 30 seconds. Remove mold and serve.

Makes 1 coffee cake.

STRAWBERRY RIPPLE TEA CAKE

Cinnamon-spiced streusel crowns this elegantly marbled sweet bread.

1¾ cup	unbleached flour	425 ml
⅔ cup	sugar	150 ml
½ tsp	ground cinnamon	½ tsp
¼ cup	butter, chilled	60 ml
2 tsp	baking powder	2 tsp
½ tsp	salt	½ tsp
¼ tsp	ground nutmeg	¼ tsp
1	egg	1
⅔ cup	milk	150 ml
¼ cup	butter, melted and cooled	60 ml
½ cup	strawberry jam	125 ml

1. In a small bowl mix ¼ cup (60 ml) of the flour, ⅓ cup (85 ml) of the sugar, and cinnamon. Cut in chilled butter until coarse crumbs form. Set aside.

2. Preheat oven to 375°F (190°C). In a large bowl stir together remaining flour and sugar, baking powder, salt, and nutmeg.

3. In a medium bowl beat egg with milk and melted butter. Add egg mixture to flour mixture, stirring until mixture is smooth. Spread batter in a prepared 8-inch (20-cm) springform pan. Spoon jam evenly over batter. Draw a knife through batter in several back-and-forth strokes to marble jam through it. Sprinkle evenly with cinnamon-sugar mixture.

4. Bake until top is well browned (40–45 minutes). Let stand 5 minutes, then remove pan sides. Serve warm.

Makes 1 tea cake.

FRUITED COFFEE CAKE

Mixed dried fruits and chopped walnuts dress up this sugar-dusted bundt cake.

⅔ cup	firmly packed brown sugar	150 ml
as needed	unbleached flour	as needed
1 tbl	ground cinnamon	1 tbl
⅓ cup	finely chopped walnuts	85 ml
8 oz	mixed dried fruits	225 g
2 tsp	baking powder	2 tsp
¼ tsp	salt	¼ tsp
¾ cup	butter, softened	175 ml
¾ cup	sugar	175 ml
1 tsp	vanilla extract	1 tsp
2	eggs	2
¾ cup	milk	175 ml
¼ cup	butter, melted and cooled	60 ml
as needed	confectioners' sugar	as needed

1. In a small bowl combine brown sugar, 1 tablespoon of the flour, cinnamon, and walnuts; mix well. Set aside.

2. Preheat oven to 350°F (175°C). Place dried fruits in a medium bowl and cover with boiling water. Let stand 10 minutes, drain, and pat dry. Chop finely.

3. In a medium bowl stir together 2 cups (500 ml) of the flour, baking powder, and salt.

4. In a large mixing bowl cream together the butter with sugar until light and fluffy. Blend in vanilla. Then add eggs, one at a time, beating well after each addition.

5. Add flour mixture to creamed mixture alternately with milk, mixing to blend after each addition. Stir in dried fruits.

6. Spoon a third of the batter into a prepared 9-inch (22.5-cm) round bundt pan. Sprinkle with half of the brown sugar mixture, then with 2 tablespoons of the melted butter. Add another third of the batter and the remaining brown sugar mixture and melted butter. Add remaining batter.

7. Bake until coffee cake is well browned (55–65 minutes). Let stand in pan on a wire rack for 15 minutes, then invert and remove pan. Cool slightly, then dust with confectioners' sugar and serve.

Makes 1 coffee cake.

SALLY LUNN, GEORGIA-STYLE

The folksy name of this famous tea bread belies its rich taste and delicate texture (see below).

½ cup	butter or shortening, softened	125 ml
½ cup	sugar	125 ml
2	eggs	2
1 cup	milk	250 ml
2 cups	cake flour, measured after sifting	500 ml
1 tbl	baking powder	1 tbl
½ tsp	salt	½ tsp

1. Heat oven to 425°F (220°C). In a small bowl cream butter and beat in sugar.

2. In a medium bowl beat eggs well, then blend with milk. In a separate large bowl combine flour, baking powder, and salt. Beat about a quarter of egg mixture into creamed butter mixture, then beat in about a quarter of the flour mixture. Repeat until all ingredients are blended and the batter is satiny.

3. Pour batter into a prepared 8-inch-square (20-cm-square) baking pan. Bake until top is golden and puffed (20–30 minutes). Cut into 2-inch (5-cm) squares and serve warm.

Makes 16 squares.

SOL ET LUNE

The French name for a quick bread that has long been a favorite in the southeastern U.S. is "Sol et Lune" (Sun and Moon). Originating in eighteenth-century France, the tea bread became popular in England. The recipe eventually found its way to colonial America, where mispronunciation resulted over time in a new name: "Sally Lunn."

COCONUT-DATE COFFEE CAKE

For a Sunday brunch, serve this tropical fruit cake with sliced oranges, omelets, and coffee.

Coconut Topping

2 tbl	unbleached flour	2 tbl
⅓ cup	firmly packed brown sugar	85 ml
½ tsp	ground cinnamon	½ tsp
2 tbl	butter, melted and cooled	2 tbl
½ cup	flaked coconut	125 ml
1½ cups	unbleached flour	350 ml
½ cup	sugar	125 ml
2 tsp	baking powder	2 tsp
½ tsp	salt	½ tsp
½ cup	chopped dates	125 ml
1	egg	1
¾ cup	milk	175 ml
¼ cup	butter, melted and cooled, or oil	60 ml

1. In a small bowl stir together flour, brown sugar, and cinnamon. Blend the 2 tablespoons melted butter with flour mixture. Stir in coconut.

2. Preheat oven to 400°F (205°C). In a large bowl stir flour, sugar, baking powder, salt, and dates.

3. In a medium bowl beat egg with milk and melted butter. Add egg mixture to flour mixture, stirring until mixture is smooth.

4. Spread batter in a prepared 8-inch-square (20-cm-square) pan. Sprinkle Coconut Topping evenly over batter. Bake until topping is golden brown (25–30 minutes). Cut into squares and serve warm.

Makes 1 coffee cake.

BLUEBERRY TEA CAKE

Dust confectioners' sugar over this almond-crusted blueberry tea cake to highlight its luscious appearance.

¼ cup each	sliced almonds and firmly packed brown sugar	60 ml each
1½ cups	unbleached flour	350 ml
¾ cup	sugar	175 ml
1 tbl	baking powder	1 tbl
½ tsp	salt	½ tsp
¼ tsp	ground nutmeg	¼ tsp
⅓ cup	butter, chilled	85 ml
1 cup	fresh blueberries	250 ml
1	egg	1
½ cup	milk	125 ml
1 tsp	vanilla extract	1 tsp
as needed	confectioners' sugar	as needed

1. Preheat oven to 350°F (175°C). Combine almonds and brown sugar; sprinkle mixture in a prepared 9-inch (22.5-cm) tube or bundt pan.

2. In a large bowl mix flour, sugar, baking powder, salt, and nutmeg; cut in butter until coarse crumbs form. Gently stir in blueberries.

3. In a small bowl beat egg lightly with milk and vanilla. Stir milk mixture into blueberry mixture, mixing just until dry ingredients are moistened.

4. Spread batter gently in prepared pan. Bake until cake is well browned (45–60 minutes). Let stand in pan for about 5 minutes, loosen edges, and invert onto a serving plate. Serve warm, dusted with confectioners' sugar.

Makes 1 tea cake.

BISCUITS, SCONES, AND MORE

The flaky biscuits, meltingly tender scones, plump popovers, crusty cream puff pastries, and charming little fry breads in this section can make your reputation as an expert baker. The quality and freshness of quick breads like these can't be duplicated by anything sold in a store.

BERRY SHORTCAKE

Shortcake is a rich relative of the humble biscuit. Strawberries are traditional with shortcake, but a mixture of fresh berries is also wonderful for this classic summer dessert. For a marbled effect, purée half the fruit and fold the purée into the whipped cream filling shortly before serving.

Shortcake

2 cups	unbleached flour	500 ml
1 tbl	baking powder	1 tbl
½ tsp	salt	½ tsp
3 tbl	sugar	3 tbl
6 tbl	butter, chilled	6 tbl
¾ cup	whipping cream	175 ml
as needed	heavy cream, for brushing tops	as needed

Berry-Cream Filling

2 pints	strawberries	900 ml
2 cups	whipping cream	500 ml
to taste	sugar	to taste
1 tsp	vanilla extract	1 tsp

1. For the shortcake, preheat oven to 425°F (220°C). Mix and cut dough into 12 rounds as for Classic Baking Powder Biscuits (see page 72). Brush tops with heavy cream and bake until golden brown (about 12 minutes).

2. For the filling, hull and slice strawberries and set aside. In a mixing bowl beat together whipping cream and sugar just until stiff. Blend in vanilla.

3. To serve, split a biscuit in half horizontally. Place the bottom on an individual serving plate. Spoon on some of the whipped cream filling and sliced berries. Cover with biscuit top. Repeat with remaining biscuits.

Makes 12 shortcakes.

CLASSIC BAKING POWDER BISCUITS

The secret of flaky biscuits is to cut in the chilled butter, using a pastry blender or two knives, until the particles are uniformly the texture of coarse crumbs (see Preparing Biscuit Dough on page 75). As the biscuits bake, the butter melts, forming tender, flaky layers. Serve these rich biscuits warm from the oven.

2 cups	unbleached flour	500 ml
1 tbl	baking powder	1 tbl
½ tsp	salt	½ tsp
½ cup	butter, chilled	125 ml
¾ cup	half-and-half or milk	175 ml
2 tbl	butter, melted and cooled	2 tbl

1. Preheat oven to 425°F (220°C). In a large bowl thoroughly mix flour, baking powder, and salt. Cut the chilled butter into flour mixture until coarse crumbs form.

2. Add half-and-half, all at once, mixing gently just until a soft dough forms. Gather dough together with your hands and transfer it to a floured board or pastry cloth. Knead gently just enough to form dough into a smooth ball; turn to coat lightly with flour.

3. Roll or pat dough out to about ½-inch (1.25-cm) thickness. Using a 2½-inch (6.25-cm) round cutter, cut dough into biscuits. Place about 1 inch (2.5 cm) apart on an ungreased baking sheet. Brush tops lightly with the melted butter.

4. Bake until biscuits are golden brown (15–20 minutes). Serve hot.

Makes 12 biscuits.

DROP BISCUITS

These biscuits are rougher in appearance than cut biscuits (see page 72) but are astonishingly easy to make. If you're in a hurry, simply drop spoonfuls of the dough, without any rolling or flouring, directly onto the baking sheet. Self-rising flour, which has salt and leavening (usually baking powder and/or baking soda) added at the mill, is a great time-saver if you bake quick breads often.

1 cup	self-rising flour	250 ml
¼ cup	butter, chilled	60 ml
½ cup	whole milk	125 ml
as needed	unbleached flour, for coating bowl	as needed

1. Preheat oven to 500°F (260°C). Put flour in a large bowl. Cut in butter until coarse crumbs form.

2. Make a well in the center of flour mixture and pour in milk. With a wooden spoon stir to make a wet, sticky dough. Beat with the spoon until milk is thoroughly integrated and dough is elastic. (Dough can be set aside at room temperature, covered, for up to an hour before baking.)

3. Place about 2 tablespoons unbleached flour in a large bowl. Use more to flour your hands. For each biscuit, scoop out a tablespoon of dough, roll lightly between your hands to the size and shape of an egg, dip on all sides in the bowl of flour, and gently drop about 1 inch (2.5 cm) apart on an oiled baking sheet.

4. Bake in top third of oven until biscuits are puffed and starting to brown (about 10 minutes). Serve warm.

Makes about 12 biscuits.

PREPARING BISCUIT DOUGH

Follow these steps for a soft dough that yields tender cut biscuits.

2. With a fork, lightly stir in liquid until mixture forms a soft dough that is still a little crumbly in texture—don't overmix.

1. Using a pastry blender or two knives, cut chilled butter or shortening into dry ingredients until flour-coated bits of fat resemble coarse crumbs.

3. Light, quick kneading (using a much gentler touch than for yeast bread) transforms the rough dough into one that can be shaped and rolled out for cutting.

ORANGE-SUGAR BISCUITS

Sprinkled with orange sugar, these rich biscuits resemble scones. They are best when served warm. See Preparing Biscuit Dough on page 75.

¼ cup	sugar	60 ml
4 tsp	grated orange zest	4 tsp
2 cups	unbleached flour	500 ml
1 tbl	baking powder	1 tbl
½ tsp	salt	½ tsp
½ cup	butter, chilled	125 ml
1	egg	1
as needed	half-and-half or milk	as needed

1. Preheat oven to 425°F (220°C). In a mixing bowl combine sugar and orange zest; remove and set aside 1 tablespoon of the mixture.

2. To sugar mixture remaining in bowl add flour, baking powder, and salt. Mix to combine dry ingredients thoroughly. Cut in butter until coarse crumbs form.

3. Beat egg with ½ cup (125 ml) of the half-and-half. Add egg mixture, all at once, to flour mixture; mix gently just until a soft dough forms. Turn dough out onto a floured board or pastry cloth, turning to coat lightly with flour. Pat or roll out to about ½ inch (1.25 cm) thick. Using a 2½-inch (6.25-cm) round cutter, cut dough into rounds. Place on an ungreased baking sheet. Brush tops lightly with half-and-half; sprinkle with reserved orange sugar.

4. Bake until golden (12–15 minutes). Serve warm.

Makes 12 biscuits.

DEEP-DISH DOUGH

Biscuit dough (see recipe on page 72) is a key ingredient in a number of deep-dish specialties. Traditional desserts like apple pandowdy, peach cobbler, and blueberry slump typically feature a blanket of biscuit dough baked over (or sometimes under) sweetened, spiced fruit. Another deep-dish favorite is chicken potpie: meaty chicken pieces and fresh vegetables in a light cream sauce, all nestled beneath a biscuit crust.

COCKTAIL SCONES

These savory rounds, made in a cocktail "mini" size, can be seasoned to order by adding 1/3 cup (85 ml) grated Parmesan or Cheddar cheese, chopped walnuts, or minced onion to the wine-egg mixture. They make a delightful mouthful on their own, or you can split them and add a filling of sliced ham or pâté.

2 cups	unbleached flour	500 ml
1 tbl	baking powder	1 tbl
½ tsp	baking soda	½ tsp
½ tsp	salt	½ tsp
½ cup	unsalted butter, chilled	125 ml
1	egg	1
½ cup	sweet wine or cream sherry	125 ml
as needed	whipping cream	as needed

1. Preheat oven to 400°F (205°C). Stir together flour, baking powder, baking soda, and salt. Cut in butter until coarse crumbs form.

2. In a small bowl whisk together egg, wine, and ⅓ cup (85 ml) of the cream. Add to dry ingredients and stir just until dry ingredients are moistened.

3. Turn dough out on a lightly floured surface and pat or roll out to about ½ inch (1.25 cm) thick. (Dough will be sticky.) Cut out 1½-inch (3.75 cm) rounds with a floured cutter.

4. Place on ungreased baking sheet. Brush tops lightly with additional cream. Bake until golden (12–15 minutes). Serve warm.

Makes about 24 scones.

CURRANT SCONES

Freshly brewed tea or coffee, lemon curd, and a brimming plateful of hot scones are a perfect beginning to a special day.

2 cups	unbleached flour	500 ml
2 tbl	sugar	2 tbl
4 tsp	baking powder	4 tsp
½ tsp	salt	½ tsp
½ cup	butter, chilled	125 ml
¾ cup	buttermilk	175 ml
¼ cup	dried currants	60 ml
as needed	butter, melted and cooled	as needed

1. Preheat oven to 425°F (220°C). In a large bowl sift together flour, sugar, baking powder, and salt. Cut the chilled butter into flour mixture until coarse crumbs form.

2. Make a well in center of flour mixture and gently stir in buttermilk and currants just until dry ingredients are moistened.

3. On a lightly floured work surface pat or roll out dough to about 1½ inches (3.75 cm) thick. Cut out scones with a round cutter or cut into squares or triangles with a knife.

4. Place on an ungreased baking sheet. Brush scones with melted butter. Bake until golden brown (about 15 minutes). Serve immediately.

Makes 12 scones.

CINNAMON SCONES

These plump, cinnamon-sugared triangles are delightful paired with tea or coffee.

2 cups	unbleached flour	500 ml
2 tsp	baking powder	2 tsp
½ tsp	baking soda	½ tsp
¼ tsp	salt	¼ tsp
½ cup	butter, chilled	125 ml
1	egg, separated	1
3 tbl	honey	3 tbl
⅓ cup	buttermilk	85 ml
1 tsp	water	1 tsp
2 tbl	sugar	2 tbl
¼ tsp	ground cinnamon	¼ tsp

1. Preheat oven to 400°F (205°C). In a large bowl stir together flour, baking powder, baking soda, and salt. Cut in butter until coarse crumbs form.

2. In a small bowl beat egg yolk with honey and buttermilk until blended. Add buttermilk mixture to flour mixture, mixing lightly just until dry ingredients are moistened.

3. With floured hands, lightly shape dough into a flattened ball. Roll out on a floured surface to a circle about ½ inch (1.25 cm) thick and 8½ inches (21.25 cm) in diameter. Using a floured knife, cut into 8 wedges. Place on an oiled baking sheet.

4. In a small bowl beat egg white slightly with water. In another bowl blend sugar and cinnamon. Brush scones lightly with egg white, then sprinkle with cinnamon sugar.

5. Bake until golden (10–12 minutes). Serve warm.

Makes about 8 scones.

DOLCI DI POLENTA

Crispy, sweet Italian cornmeal rounds, full of wine-drenched currants, provide a memorable finish to a summer meal. Note that the dough must chill for an hour before baking.

1 cup	cornmeal	250 ml
1¾ cups	unbleached flour	425 ml
½ tsp	baking powder	½ tsp
pinch	salt	pinch
6 tbl	mascarpone or cream cheese	6 tbl
10 tbl	unsalted butter, softened	10 tbl
½ cup	sugar	125 ml
1	egg	1
½ tsp	almond extract	½ tsp
½ tsp	vanilla extract	½ tsp
½ cup	dried currants soaked in Marsala for 1 hour and drained	125 ml

1. Sift together cornmeal, flour, baking powder, and salt. Set aside.

2. In a large mixing bowl cream the cheese and butter until blended. Add sugar and beat until light and fluffy. Add egg, almond and vanilla extracts, and beat until well blended. Add currants and mix to incorporate. Add cornmeal mixture and mix to blend.

3. Form dough into 2 rolls, each 2 inches (5 cm) in diameter. Wrap each roll in plastic wrap or foil and freeze 1 hour or chill 4–5 hours.

4. Preheat oven to 350°F (175°C). Cut rolls into slices ⅜ inch (1 cm) thick and place ½ inch (1.25 cm) apart on prepared baking sheets.

5. Bake until lightly browned (about 16–18 minutes). Cool on racks and store in airtight containers for up to one week.

Makes about 48 biscuits.

POPOVERS FOR TWO

Light-as-air popovers rely on trapped steam, not leavening, to make them puff up. They are best made shortly before you're planning to serve them and enjoyed while they're hot. This recipe can easily be doubled or tripled.

½ cup	sifted unbleached flour	125 ml
⅛ tsp	salt	⅛ tsp
½ cup	milk	125 ml
2 tbl	butter, melted and cooled	2 tbl
1	egg, lightly beaten	1

1. Place an ungreased popover or muffin pan in oven and preheat to 450°F (230°C). In a small bowl whisk together flour, salt, milk, and melted butter until smooth. Gently whisk in egg. Fill 2 of the cups in preheated popover or custard cups half full with batter. Do not overfill or popovers will develop a dense, muffinlike texture.

2. Bake popovers in center of middle rack of oven for 15 minutes. Reduce heat to 350°F (175°C); bake another 20 minutes, until puffed and golden brown. The crust should be firm, not soft or soggy. Do not open oven door during baking. Serve at once.

Makes 2 popovers.

PREPARING A PROPER POPOVER

Making a proper popover—the American cousin to Yorkshire pudding—calls for bakeware that absorbs heat well, such as cast iron or tinned steel. Rich with egg and butter, popover batter rises best in ungreased, preheated pans. As the batter hits the hot surface of the pan, a jolt of heat and steam is released, forcing the batter to expand rapidly and form the distinctive crisp shell surrounding a pocket of air.

CHEESE PUFF RING

Cream puff pastry (see Making Cream Puff Pastry on page 88) makes a toothsome cheese-flavored bread to serve as an appetizer or a salad accompaniment. This particular pastry is a traditional specialty from the Burgundy region of France.

1 cup	milk	250 ml
¼ cup	butter	60 ml
½ tsp	salt	½ tsp
to taste	ground nutmeg and cayenne pepper	to taste
1 cup	unbleached flour	250 ml
4	eggs	4
1 cup	grated Gruyère or Swiss cheese	250 ml

1. Preheat oven to 375°F (190°C). In a saucepan combine milk and butter. Place over medium heat and cook, stirring occasionally, until butter melts. Add salt, nutmeg, and cayenne.

2. Add flour all at once, stirring until mixture leaves sides of pan and forms a ball (about 2 minutes). Remove pan from heat.

3. Beat in eggs, one at a time, beating after each addition until mixture is smooth and glossy. Stir in ¾ cup (175 ml) of the cheese.

4. Spoon dough into 8 equal mounds, placed slightly apart, in the shape of a ring on an oiled baking sheet. Sprinkle with remaining cheese.

5. Bake until puffs are well browned and crisp (40–45 minutes). Serve hot.

Makes 1 pastry ring.

MAKING CREAM PUFF PASTRY

Cream Puff Pastry (see Cheese Puff Ring on page 86) is well-suited to entertaining because it freezes beautifully. Prepare the dough in advance, shape it, then wrap airtight in plastic wrap and freeze. Shaped dough can be baked directly from the freezer before the guests arrive. Unshaped pastry dough should defrost in the refrigerator overnight, or for four hours at room temperature, before shaping and baking. The finished pastry will be light and flaky.

2. Add eggs, one at a time, beating after each addition. The paste will separate into lumps after the addition of each egg. When stirred vigorously, the paste will return to a smooth consistency. The mixture is ready to be spooned onto a baking sheet when it becomes smooth and shiny. It should be stiff enough to hold its shape when spooned.

1. After adding flour to butter mixture in saucepan, cook over medium heat, stirring vigorously until mixture pulls away from sides of pan, forms a ball, and leaves a white film on saucepan. Remove from heat; cool 5 minutes.

CHURROS

Made from "ropes" of cream puff pastry, churros (see photo on page 91) are a crisp, golden fry bread popular in Mexico.

1 cup	water	250 ml
½ tsp	salt	½ tsp
1 tbl	sugar	1 tbl
½ cup	butter	125 ml
1 cup	unbleached flour	250 ml
4	eggs	4
as needed	oil, for frying	as needed
as needed	Cinnamon Sugar (see page 30)	as needed

1. Place water, salt, sugar, and butter in a heavy saucepan. Heat slowly until butter melts, then bring to a full boil.

2. Add flour all at once, and beat vigorously until the mixture is thick and smooth. Continue beating over medium heat for about 2 minutes, then remove.

3. Using a hand-held electric mixer, add eggs, one at a time, beating well after each addition until mixture is smooth.

4. In a frying kettle heat 2 inches (5 cm) of oil to 390°F (200°C). Scoop mixture into a large pastry bag fitted with a ½-inch (1.25-cm) star tip and fold down top of the bag to seal.

5. Squeeze bag over the hot oil, pushing out a rope of pastry 4 inches (10 cm) long. Cut with a knife, letting rope fall gently into oil. Rapidly form about 6 more churros the same way. Turn them frequently until golden (about 2 minutes). Remove with a slotted spoon and drain on paper towels. Fry remaining dough the same way, and while churros are still warm, toss them in Cinnamon Sugar.

Makes about 36 churros.

BUÑUELOS

Buñuelos, often available in Mexican bakeries, are small puffs of sweet dough, so light and airy it's hard to stop eating them.

¼ cup	butter, softened	60 ml
⅓ cup	sugar	85 ml
2	eggs	2
1 tsp	vanilla extract	1 tsp
1¾ cups	unbleached flour	425 ml
2 tsp	baking powder	2 tsp
1 tsp	salt	1 tsp
¼ cup	milk	60 ml
as needed	oil, for frying	as needed
as needed	Cinnamon Sugar (see page 30)	as needed

1. In a medium mixing bowl cream together butter and sugar until blended. Add eggs and beat well. Stir in vanilla.

2. Sift 1 cup (250 ml) of the flour with baking powder and salt. Add to first mixture and mix just until dry ingredients are moistened. Beat in milk. Add the remaining flour and mix to make a soft dough.

3. Turn onto a floured surface and knead until dough is smooth (about 2 minutes), adding more flour as necessary to keep dough from being too sticky.

4. Roll dough until it is about ¼ inch (.6 cm) thick, flouring it lightly if it sticks. Using a 3-inch (7.5-cm) cutter, cut into rounds.

5. In a frying kettle, heat about 2 inches (5 cm) of oil to 360°F (180°C). Fry about 6 buñuelos at a time, turning them often, until puffy and golden (about 2 minutes). Drain on paper towels and toss in Cinnamon Sugar while still warm.

Makes about 24 buñuelos.

SOPAIPILLAS

Popular in the Southwest, these "little pillows" of fried dough can be served for breakfast, at dinner, or even for dessert. Chill the dough overnight for easy handling.

2 cups	unbleached flour	500 ml
½ tsp	salt	½ tsp
2 tsp	baking powder	2 tsp
2 tsp	sugar	2 tsp
2 tbl	lard or shortening	2 tbl
½ cup	hot water	125 ml
as needed	oil	as needed
as needed	confectioners' sugar	as needed
as needed	honey	as needed

1. Sift together flour, salt, baking powder, and sugar. With a pastry blender or two knives, cut in lard to make a lumpy meal. Add water, stirring with a fork, until a dough forms. Flour hands and rapidly knead the dough about 12 times. If the dough sticks, add flour by tablespoons and knead it in until the dough is easily handled. If dough is too crumbly and dry to knead, add more hot water by tablespoons. After kneading, cover dough with plastic wrap and let stand at room temperature for 30 minutes, or refrigerate overnight.

2. Heat oven to 325°F (160°C). Pour at least 1½ inches (3.75 cm) of oil into a frying kettle and heat to 375°F (190°C). Meanwhile, on a floured surface roll out dough in a rectangle about ¼ inch (.6 cm) thick. Cut dough into 3-inch (7.5-cm) squares. Drop squares into hot oil, a few at a time. The squares will fall, then rise as they puff into "pillows." Push them down and turn often until they are golden. Remove with a slotted spoon, drain on paper towels, and keep warm in oven. Dust with confectioners' sugar and serve with honey.

Makes about 16 sopaipillas.

NAVAHO FRY BREAD

Uncooked, the dough rounds look like thick tortillas. Just before you fry them, poke a small hole in the middle of each round to keep the center from puffing.

2 cups	unbleached flour	500 ml
1 tbl	baking powder	1 tbl
1 tsp	salt	1 tsp
1 tbl	lard or shortening	1 tbl
1 cup	boiling water	250 ml
2 cups	oil	500 ml

1. Combine flour, baking powder, and salt. Cut in lard. Make well in center. Pour boiling water into flour mixture and stir until mixture forms a ball. Cover with plastic wrap and allow to rest at room temperature for 45 minutes, or refrigerate up to one week.

2. Take a lump of dough about the size of a lime and lightly sprinkle with flour. Place dough on floured surface and press with the heel of your hand to form a slightly flattened round. Sprinkle flour on both sides of the round and roll out to a rough circle about 5 inches (12.5 cm) in diameter. Repeat with remaining dough. Place each circle on lightly floured waxed paper until ready to fry.

3. In a frying kettle, heat oil to 375°F (190°C). Just before frying poke a small hole in the center of each round of dough. Fry rounds, one by one, until they are browned, puffed, and crisp (about 2 minutes per side), turning with tongs halfway through cooking. Drain on paper towels. Serve hot.

Makes about 8 rounds.

INDEX